Foreword by Tom Inglis

The SEED Of LOVE

Loving God's Way

PAMELA A. SEGNERI

The Seed Of Love - Loving God's Way

Copyright © 2024 - Pamela Segneri

All rights reserved. This book is protected by the copyright laws of Australia. This book may not be copied or reprinted for commercial gain or profit. The use of short quotations or occasional page copying for personal or group study is permitted and encouraged provided the source is acknowledged. Permission will be granted upon request. Unless otherwise identified, Scripture quotations are taken from the New American Standard Bible® NASB® Copyright © 1960, 1971, 1977, 1995, 2020 by The Lockman Foundation. Used by permission. All rights reserved. www.Lockman.org. Scripture quotations marked TPT are from The Passion Translation®. Copyright © 2017 by BroadStreet Publishing® Group, LLC. Used by permission. All rights reserved. thePassionTranslation.com. Scripture quotations marked NKJV are from The Holy Bible, New King James Version. Copyright © 1982 by Thomas Nelson, Inc. Used by permission. All rights reserved. www.thenkjvbible.com. Emphasis with Scripture quotations is the author's own. Please note that Mountain Train Media's publishing style capitalizes certain pronouns in Scripture that refer to the Father, Son, and Holy Spirit, and may differ from some Bible publishers' styles. Take note that the name satan and related names are not capitalized. We choose not to acknowledge him, even to the point of violating grammatical rules.

Published by Mountain Train Media
QLD, Australia
publishing@mountaintrainmedia.com.au
www.mountaintrainmedia.com.au

ISBN: 978-0-6453782-4-5

Dedication

This is of course for the Lord Jesus Christ without whom I would have no idea of Love.

To my precious family;

Paul, my husband without whom I wouldn't be where I am today. His belief in me and unconditional love for me is astounding.

To our sons Simon and Todd, Simon's wife Nikita and our remarkable grandchildren - Shaikhani, Teah, Mia, Lilli and George.

My brother Graham, his wife Irene and their daughters Elisha and Laura.

My other nieces Vicki, Samantha, Sarah and Maren.

Each one of these family members bring something unique to my life.

I also dedicate this to the true friends who are as family to us. These precious ones whom the Lord brought into our lives truly fulfilling the Word; 'a friend is a gift from God'.

4 THE SEED OF LOVE

Acknowledgements

As with any project there have been many who have encouraged and assisted along the way.

I want to especially acknowledge the tireless work of my husband Paul, his editing and design skills have been a gift.

Thank you to our dear friend Tom Inglis for writing the foreword.

With this book it is so much more than print on paper it's about life (as I hope all my books are). In response to that I acknowledge my parents and grandparents who modelled unconditional God kind of love, that for me is invaluable. To Jack and Mya who probably taught me more about unconditional love than I knew at the time.

To my dear friends Bruce and Cheryl Lindley, Barb Krueger and Robyn Martin - thank you for your love and encouragement along the way.

I also would like to acknowledge my friend Raya who has interceded for us faithfully for many years and suggested I should write the Seed Of Love. So here it is!

6 THE SEED OF LOVE

Contents

Foreword: Tom Inglis....p9

Introduction....p13

Chapter 1: This Thing Called Love....p15

Chapter 2: The Greatest Gift Of All....p23

Chapter 3: Love Never Fails - 1 Corinthians 13....p31

Chapter 4: So What Is The Seed?....p41

Chapter 5: Love And Loss....p49

Chapter 6: Love Dismantles The Works Of The Enemy....p57

Chapter 7: It's A Choice....p61

Chapter 8: Nothing Is Impossible....p67

Chapter 9: Eternal Life....p73

Chapter 10: The Last Word....p79

8 THE SEED OF LOVE

Foreword

When reading this book, I felt that I was sitting in the same room listening to Pamela speak personally to me, partly because I know her as a woman of sincere faith and love for God. The book reflects Pamela's mature insight and prophetic understanding into the most important subject in the Bible – the Love of God. There's a sincerity in her penmanship that leaves the reader encouraged but also challenged to pursue the Love of God, and particularly to meditate on the Father's Love for each of His children. I think she highlights the Love of the Father that draws the reader to trust Him in a relational way that many readers may not have considered.

Pamela unequivocally shows us that all our efforts in the Christian life are wasted if we do not operate from a foundation of love. She affirms that everything God has given us as an inheritance including the Gifts of the Spirit can only find their fullest expression through lovers of God. The potential of both personal and Kingdom advancement can only be achieved with a solid understanding and practical outpouring of God's Love flowing through us.

The book is a clarion call for the Church to be awake and aware in the hour in which we live, and how our greatest asset to overcome the challenges that lie before us is to operate in the Love of God. It's a prophetic call and reminder to all of us that if we exercise Love in our daily walk, our future is secure.

We are on the cusp of a great outpouring of unprecedented power that the prophets of old only caught a glimpse of. This book is an inspirational call to remind us that God's agenda for the Church must be an outpouring of Agape Love. The simplicity of the message is matched by the power of the truth it carries, that "Love never fails".

If you are passionate about God's master plan and walk in it, then this book is for you.

Enjoy!

Pastor Tom Inglis B.Min M.Sc

Founder of Psalmody International

11

12 THE SEED OF LOVE

Introduction

This book is offered to inspire, challenge, provoke and bless each and everyone whose hands it comes into.

This has been a lifetime of discovery of 'what is this thing called Love?'

In fact there are different kinds of Love which will all bring a different harvest however that is another revelation.

So which seed have I planted? Is it the seed for my desired harvest?

14   THE SEED OF LOVE

CHAPTER 1

This Thing Called Love

For God so loved the world that He gave…..

Right there in John 3:16 is where it generally starts for a Believer in Christ. But is that where it really starts?

Let's look at the story of creation in Genesis 1:1 - Genesis 2:3

My thought is that God is Love and I hope we can all agree on that point. He desired to show that Love and did so as He created the Heavens and the Earth, the birds of the air, the fish of the sea, the animals and plants. I believe He had a great desire to reproduce. He therefore created man in His image to lavish Himself and His bountiful Love upon.

The first act of that unconditional love was that He gave man dominion over every creature. Please note that Adam wasn't given dominion over mankind - this is an important point to remember.

> ***Then God said, "Let Us make mankind in Our image, according to Our likeness; and let them rule over the fish of the sea and over the birds of the sky and over the livestock and over all the earth, and over every crawling thing that crawls on the earth." Genesis 1:26***

For God so loved His creation that He gave.

Everyone on earth believes they understand love. There have been books and poems written, movies produced and many songs sung highlighting mankind's great knowledge, need and understanding of love.

For myself, I believed that until I understood more of God Our Loving Father, I truly didn't understand love at all.

There are so many expressions of this thing called love. In fact the Greek language breaks love down into seven categories, as opposed to the English where we only have the one word LOVE.

Below we are unpacking these and yes we only have four below, the other three definitions are repeats of these.

Phileo is the brotherly love. The love we have for a friend. The love we must display for others. Phileo maybe characterised as the warm and fuzzy feeling we all feel from time to time, and it is just that. It may be difficult to Phileo someone when they let you down. Newsflash - people will always let us down! Just as we will sooner or later let them down. These disappointments may or may not be related to any genuine wrong doing. Often it is simply our perception and/or expectation. However, because Phileo is dependant on everyone holding hands, sitting around a campfire singing 'cum by ya' - that relationship may be broken beyond repair.

Eros is the sexual love often known as lust, as it is more about self gratification. Please know in the context of our Heavenly Father sexuality and the act itself is not bad or sinful. After all God created it!

The problem arises when we leave God out of the equation. Please understand this is most certainly not about judgement, we have all just operated with the information we had at the time. When we are whole and completely yielded to God in this area this sexual love is the doorway to greater intimacy with our spouse and God.

Philautia is one we seldom characterise and yet we see it all around us all day everyday. Philautia is self love which may be characterised as idolatry of self or worst case scenario, narcicism. Right now the pendulum of society seems to have swung back to the behaviours of the great civilisations of the past. Historically, every great society has been destroyed because this type of love is out of balance. This can also be said of a societal downfall due to an inbalance of Eros. Essentially every hedonistic desire or pursuit is sanctioned by this.

I am not against gym memberships or spas or nail salons or eyelash extensions or in fact makeup and skincare and cosmetic surgeons. The issue is when these things are completely out of balance with the entirety of our lives.

When our self worth is not found in Christ but rather how many likes, follows, shares etc we have on the various social media platforms. The sinister side of this is we become prey for people who don't know us personally and probably never will. They may become an extremely loud voice in our head. Then because of the nature of these things people love to share and add to these foul, nasty comments. It's that old thing, people cannot look away from a car crash. There is a perversity that is aroused as someone is experiencing possibly the worst day of their lives and social media may also arouse that.

Philautia is the love that tells us and anyone who will listen that we are in fact the centre of the universe.

This may be the root of Narcissism. It has no care for others, no empathy which of course may lead to much more serious behavioural issues.

There is nothing wrong with self care, our body is the temple of the Holy Spirit and it would therefore be wise to keep it in good repair.

Everything is about balance.

Now **Agape** is the God kind of Love. The true unconditional love out of which all other expressions of love freely flow.

That is my premise - Agape is the true seed of Love. This should be the place from which every other relationship and pursuit flows.

I know that this may not always be an easy thing, there must be a total yielding to the Lord. Trusting that if we

> **..*seek first the kingdom of God and His righteousness, and ALL THESE THINGS shall be added to you.* Matthew 6:33** *(emphasis is mine)*

That is one of the great promises that has been given to us. So what are 'all these things'? EVERYTHING! All is all, if it wasn't all Jesus would have said SOME of these things and yet He didn't. Our loving heavenly Father did not put limits on anything that He gave us and there are no boundaries around Gods goodness -

unless we place them there!

If you have trouble fathoming unconditional love start here;

If you are a parent, remember when you held that child and they looked at you. You can see that deep trust in their eyes. We see that even with little children who have been treated badly, they are still ready to unconditionally love their caregiver. As we regard our loving Father, we too must recapture that wonder, that overwhelming flood of more than emotion. It is something on a spiritual level - it is that God kind of Love.

We are believers in the Lord Jesus and He looks at us all day everyday just like that. When He hung on the cross I believe He looked through time and saw each of us. Then He gave up His spirit so we could be snatched out of the enemy's clutches. If you're still not seeing it perhaps you have had a dog (or possibly a cat) and as a tiny puppy or kitten they looked up at you and you were it for them, love and trust that was unfathomable.

Once we begin to reflect that Agape Love all around us the other three (or six if you're a purist) come into correct focus so every other one flows out of the one true source.

Plant it in your life today, water it and nurture it.

This is the Seed of Love!

22   THE SEED OF LOVE

CHAPTER 2

The Greatest Gift Of All

And now abide faith, hope, love, these three; but the greatest of these is love.
1 Corinthians 13:13 (NKJV)

I suspect Paul knew a thing or two about this, probably because he had failed so badly in his pre Christ life. Let me hasten to add he faltered and often failed as many of us have.

The scriptures are given to us for our correction, reproof, admonishment and instruction. That is I believe why so many of the great Bible heroes missed the mark before they received revelation and subsequently succeeded. They were like us - human. In that humanity, regardless of the current circumstances we must see the possibility and potential for us to fulfil our destiny in Christ.

Bob Jones had a death experience in 1975 in which he had a transformational experience with God. I am not going to go into that here as you can find it for yourself to see the full extent of that experience.

What I am interested in is The Father's question to each one as they approached Him.

"Did you learn to love?"

Such a simple inquiry, yet it struck me as something quite profound in it's simplicity. The key word was learn. Did you learn to love?

I don't know about you but I don't recall a class on love in school. Even more interesting, I don't recall being taught to love at Sunday school. I think maybe it was inferred but was that good enough?

The fruit of the Spirit in Galatians 5:22-23 reads;

> **But the fruit of the Spirit is love, joy, peace, patience, kindness, goodness, faithfulness, gentleness, self-control; against such things there is no law.**

I guess like so many issues in scripture it is assumed because you prayed a sinners prayer and then you were baptised in the Spirit, you automatically have it all.

Yet here was our Heavenly Father asking the

question of the ages, "Did you learn to love?"

This has to be important! My experience with God, Jesus and Holy Spirit is that they do not waste words.

So my question to you is have you learned to love?

Second question, how do you learn to love?

The third question is just as important as the other two. Which love is God talking about?

Now before you slam the book down and label me as something uncomplimentary, hear me out.

In the beginning Adam and Eve walked in the garden in perfect harmony with God and each other. In fact with all creation, everything was a tangible experience of love. God's overwhelming, all encompassing love.

Then as we read on, we all know the story, satan in the form of a serpent seduced Eve with the empty promise of being like God. He introduced doubt to Eve. Doubt about God's intentions and that was enough. She sold Adam on this great new revelation that they could be like God by eating this fruit. (I will resist the urge to editorialise at this point.)

What I would like you to see is they already had perfect love with God, each other and their environment. When satan introduced doubt around God's motives - everything changed.

The perfect love, which was all that they had known and enjoyed was fractured.

As we have come through the generations, that perfect love has been lost to us. Please note that even though God drove Adam and Eve out of the Garden of Eden, He still loved them. This is evidenced by Genesis 3:21

And the LORD God made garments of skin for Adam and his wife, and clothed them.

He did not want them to be uncovered so He provided covering for them as He did for us with Christ. That great compassionate love is almost impossible for us to comprehend. The hurt that God must have felt was covered by His Agape Love for His creation.

Hatred stirs up strife, But love covers all sins. Proverbs 10:12 NKJV

God's heart right back in the garden was for restoration and reconciliation. He had no time for hatred or anger towards His creation only love. Now you may cite instances in the Word where God was angry and destroyed and that is valid. However, God was destroying His enemies not His creation. This is why it is so important we remember that we do not fight against flesh and blood but rather principalities and powers (dark spiritual forces).

Jesus came to reconnect us to the Father if we choose to reconcile with Him. This reconnection was miraculous, Jesus through the cross bridged the gap between God and man. That great chasm that had opened up due to deception and rebellion in the garden had a bridge built to span the gap on that day.

> *Therefore if anyone is in Christ, this person is a new creation; the old things passed away; behold, new things have come.*
> 2 Corinthians 5:17

This scripture is of course absolutely true. Sometimes God miraculously infuses us with love and we maybe instantly changed in that regard. Yet due to the thousands of years of man's estrangement from God there are perhaps things that we must unlearn or be delivered of. We must never forget or overlook the power of the 2 Corinthians revelation. We are legally new creations and should approach all things from that perspective of victory.

It therefore follows we must learn the ways of God as we grow in relationship with Him. We cannot leave a void or the familiar spirits will return in force.

Perhaps the most fundamental errors in many peoples Christian upbringing is the misunderstanding of love. We were taught to reverence God above all else and there is nothing incorrect about reverence however, the way it was framed in my understanding was fear, not faith and most certainly not love.

This taught the people who were trying to relate and draw close to God as their Father that He was in fact far off. He was unapproachable in a manner we understood. The result being that we were all waiting for the other shoe to drop as it were. If things were too good and we didn't deserve it so the correction of heaven was going to fall on us and that would mean pain and probably loss. Our fallen human condition had taught us to expect pain. No one and nothing would be loving, gentle and kind toward us because we weren't good enough we weren't worth it. That spirit of unworthiness is very real and shapes and misdirects so many peoples lives.

The truth that 'God loved us' that we received as revelation when we were 'Born Again', was only a momentary flash. Often times the back up teaching we received as young believers was about doctrine and the sacraments all of which are important and yet secondary to the truth about love.

To know our Father in heaven loves us was quite a foreign concept to many of us. To imagine He was intimately concerned with every facet of our lives and in particular my life, was a little mind blowing. It was therefore easier for so many of us to believe that the Fear of God was terror rather than awe.

As a child brought up in church, my revelation was that Jesus was loving and good and kind whilst God sat up in heaven on His throne waiting to dole out punishment.

So many of us loved God yet were wary of Him!

I believe this is a God inspired line that I have used often 'He is Jehovah Jireh not Jehovah Jarrah.'

Just to explain, in Australia where I grew up Jarrah is a hardwood. So God was not sitting in heaven with a big stick, He had open arms and an open heart to listen to us and provide for us.

Religion taught us that God was far off - Love brought Him near!

30 THE SEED OF LOVE

CHAPTER 3

Love Never Fails
1 Corinthians 13

As part of marriage ceremonies across the globe, (some of them Christian and some not) this chapter from the New Testament is regularly read.

As I have sat in observation I have often wondered at how and indeed why this is being read, decreed, and prophesied over this couple. It is as though the reading of this is some magic incantation that will transform the couple from who they are to whom all the well wishers would like them to be.

Now I believe the Word is transforming but not because someone waved a Bible over your head. It transforms us as we believe what the Lord Jesus is actually communicating to us in this Word. If you have read 'The Seed of Faith' you will know I absolutely believe that; 'faith comes by hearing and hearing by the word of God'. So I am not completely discounting the value of reading the chapter I am just saying as this dewy eyed couple gaze upon each other I am not sure how much hearing is actually going on. For most couples the wedding is a blur, I guess that is reasonable when the production has taken many months, sometimes years to plan and has to be pulled off with military precision.

Now my belief is that this passage of scripture is for our entire life. This is something we should holdfast to regardless of our family situation or current circumstances.

> *Though I speak with the tongues of men and of angels, but have not love, I have become sounding brass or a clanging cymbal.*
> 1 Corinthians 13:1 NKJV

It is more than just having eloquent speech or an engaging turn of phrase. The words we speak must bring life - Love brings life!

> *And though I have the gift of prophecy, and understand all mysteries and all knowledge, and though I have all faith, so that I could remove mountains, but have not love, I am nothing.*
> 1 Corinthians 13:2 NKJV

There is no point in moving in all the great gifts that Holy Spirit can release if we do not have love. Your gift may take you where your character won't keep you!

> *And though I bestow all my goods to feed the poor, and though I give my body to be burned, but have not love, it profits me nothing.*
> 1 Corinthians 13:3 NKJV

The Aramaic translated here as burn also means boast. We must be careful that everything aforementioned is undertaken because of love and not self promotion.

> *Love suffers long and is kind; love does not envy; love does not parade itself, is not puffed up*
> 1 Corinthians 13:4 NKJV

I read a commentary note on this verse which I love. It reads, 'Love transforms the spirit'.

> *does not behave rudely, does not seek its own, is not provoked, thinks no evil*
> 1 Corinthians 13:5 NKJV

Love will overlook offences and remain laser focussed on what is good, always refusing to hold any resentment.

does not rejoice in iniquity, but rejoices in the truth 1 Corinthians 13:6 NKJV

Always rejoicing finding joy in the truth which is Jesus our Lord.

bears all things, believes all things, hopes all things, endures all things.
1 Corinthians 13:7 NKJV

The word translated as 'bears' may also be translated as it is in Mark 2:4 as 'roof'. So it is reasonable to understand this as; Love is the roof over all things. Love covers all things and will protect and shield.

Love never fails. But whether there are prophecies, they will fail; whether there are tongues, they will cease; whether there is knowledge, it will vanish away.
1 Corinthians 13:8 NKJV

Love never falters, it is steady and consistent. It is important to note that the knowledge mentioned here is the Holy Spirit gift of words of knowledge. It is not knowledge in general as our knowledge of God will not pass away, rather it will grow and deepen.

For we know in part and we prophesy in part.
1 Corinthians 13:9 NKJV

This side of heaven we may have fragments of a vision or revelation. The exciting thing for the body of

Christ is we all have a different fragment but together we have the possibility of seeing the complete picture.

But when that which is perfect has come, then that which is in part will be done away.
1 Corinthians 13:10 NKJV

Perfect love diminishes the importance of all else. Their importance including the Holy Spirit's gifts, will all be displaced by perfect Love.

When I was a child, I spoke as a child, I understood as a child, I thought as a child; but when I became a man, I put away childish things.
1 Corinthians 13:11 NKJV

Here Paul is admonishing us, we must grow in wisdom and mature in all things.

For now we see in a mirror, dimly, but then face to face. Now I know in part, but then I shall know just as I also am known.
1 Corinthians 13:12 NKJV

The transforming perfect love of God will bring us as Numbers 12:7-8 says;

"It is not this way for My servant Moses; He is faithful in all My household; With him I speak mouth to mouth, That is, openly, and not using mysterious language....

No longer through dreams and figures of speech - mouth to mouth. Our conversation and relationship with Father God becomes clear and open.

> *And now abide faith, hope, love, these three; but the greatest of these is love.*
> 1 Corinthians 13:13 NKJV

Everything springs from love therefore love is the greatest.

That is a lot to consider. As I said before, this is for our whole lives and not simply for a wedding service.

It addresses for me the weightiness of the 'new commandment' Jesus gave.

> *I am giving you a new commandment, that you love one another; just as I have loved you, that you also love one another.*
> John 13:34

For me, the next verse is even more powerful.

> *By this all people will know that you are My disciples: if you have love for one another."*
> John 13:35

We understand this, the whole world will know we are His. It's almost too simple, yet incredibly difficult to achieve. This is why it is imperative we are to renew our minds daily.

We must stop thinking the way the world would have us to think; love is weak therefore you are a pushover. It takes great strength of character to love the way 1 Corinthians 13 would have us love.

That is why it is important to allow the Seed of Love time and opportunity to grow and flourish. Just like a plant, if it is not thriving in the conditions - change the conditions!

I encourage you to meditate on 1 Corinthians 13 and see what Holy Spirit would reveal to you.

The gifts that God gives us are wonderful and powerful yet Love is greater why? Because we can never minister the gifts the way Jesus desires unless we are operating in love.

Love never fails! Love always wins!

As I pondered on that statement I knew there was a deeper meaning. A friend of mine sent me a quote she had found which brought my thoughts into focus.

"Love is never wasted, for its value does not rest upon reciprocity." ___ C.S. Lewis

As we love with the love God Himself has birthed within us it is we who change. Our character is being changed, indeed moulded into His character. Therefore the outcome our love had hoped for is no longer our goal, the love of God coursing through us releases the outcome into His hands.

We must never forget God gave each one of us on the planet (not just the Christians) a free will. He cannot and will not change our minds. It is only as we yield to the work which Holy Spirit is doing within us that our minds change.

> **And do not be conformed to this world, but be transformed by the renewing of your mind, so that you may prove what the will of God is, that which is good and acceptable and perfect.**
> *Romans 12:2*

That is absolutely our choice.

Prayer, birthed in Love and prayed by Faith changes things. So we never stop and we never quit!

So I repeat;

Love never fails!

Love always wins!

40   THE SEED OF LOVE

CHAPTER 4

So What Is The Seed?

So just as with every other thing your seed is of the utmost importance. That is why it is imperative that we understand love. Real Love - the God kind of Love.

God loved us before we were in our mothers womb. He had actually conceived us prior to it manifesting. He knew what we would look like, what gender we would be, our strengths and our challenges. The plans and dreams for our lives, our destiny was all written by God onto the scroll of our life on earth.

That's the love seed we need to plant in our lives. The perfect Father love, unconditional yet never weak. The love that would shape our lives for eternity.

Now let me hasten to add that much has been written about Father love, father hurts and so on. I am not going to add to that revelation. I only mention it to underline the importance of the right seed.

It is so easy to focus on what you may not have had from your natural father. How much better it is to meditate on what you do have everyday freely available to you from our Heavenly Father.

As we begin to understand our identity in Christ everything changes. The things that have hurt and disappointed do nothing but keep us earthbound, that is to say under the circumstances. We attract all kinds of extra negativity, hurts and disappointments that were never necessarily part of the original hurt.

The good news however is the God kind of love if we allow it, will multiply and grow. This love gives us access to the kingdom of God in ways we previously could never imagine.

Love grows - it's a seed! Plant it in your heart and allow it to do what it was created to do - Increase.

Let us be a people who represent The Father, The Son (the Lord Jesus Christ) and The Holy Spirit by our love.

Remember; Love is never weak. It takes true strength to love the God way!

Seed of Love

When we talk about seeds, encapsulated within that seed pod is everything that we expect to manifest as they ripen and come to harvest. Every promise, every potential and every possibility!

As we talk about the Seed of Love we have to consider exactly what seed we are planting, just as we would when planting any type of seed. We have already looked at the various types of love so the question we must ask is essentially what harvest do we want to reap?

When talking about seeds, it's natural to look at plants. There are many plants within the same family and yet they are completely diverse. Some, whilst very beautiful to regard are in fact toxic. If we were to consider that in the light of Love; we should ask what love are we sowing?

Sometimes what we think is love may not be the love we want to bear fruit in the future. For example; when our children are small many of us wanted to almost smother them. As they grow we want to protect them of course and then call that love. Now that kind of love may not produce the harvest we desire. If this way of smothering and overprotecting is our style of love it may not be encouraging our children to grow. We want them to grow into strong, independent adults which as well adjusted parents should be our desired outcome. The smothering overprotective love may stymie their growing independence.

The same could be said of the 'Tough Love' concept. It's wise to exercise all good things in moderation.

Look at the following verses.

> *A false balance is an abomination to the LORD, But a just weight is His delight.*
> *Proverbs 11:1*

> *Diverse weights are an abomination to the LORD, And dishonest scales are not good.*
> *Proverbs 20:23* NKJV

So in all things we need to be balanced, we need to be looking towards the harvest in whatever we are sowing today. Remembering always; whatever we are doing is in fact sowing, we are constantly sowing in word and deed. Most times it is the unconscious sowing that we must be most aware of. We need to keep eternity in mind.

'Tough Love' would maybe seem like the perfect antidote for a difficult child/teenagers behaviour. Yet as tempting as that is it can be cruel.

The one thing we should never be towards a child is cruel because we are teaching them a behaviour style that we may not relish when the harvest ripens.

Tough Love is never an excuse for cruelty. Love is firm and unwavering with the boundaries that have been put in place.

We have raised two sons and have had the privilege of being very involved in the raising of three of our granddaughters. I only say that so you can see this is not academic for me. Through the most challenging times Holy Spirit constantly reminded me of the father of the prodigal son. It wasn't wasted on him what his son had done it just didn't matter. For him as for us; love, restoration and reconciliation are far more important.

So back to seed, we must be mindful of the harvest we are sowing to.

> *Grace and peace be multiplied to you in the knowledge of God and of Jesus our Lord, for His divine power has granted to us everything pertaining to life and godliness, through the true knowledge of Him who called us by His own glory and excellence. Through these He has granted to us His precious and magnificent promises, so that by them you may become partakers of the divine nature, having escaped the corruption that is in the world on account of lust.*
> *2 Peter 1:2-4*

46 THE SEED OF LOVE

The God seed is already planted within us. It is up to us to accept and nurture it or let it wither and die.

48 THE SEED OF LOVE

CHAPTER 5

Love and Loss

Once a seed is planted there is always great expectation. As we water and nurture we are looking forward to the day that we see fruit forming and then harvest.

It is the potential that is in the seed. From one seed many fields can be planted and harvested. Sadly, we know that is not always the case.

Whatever the type of seed, once planted it must be cared for. It is important to note that different seeds need different care.

So to the Seed of Love; it is delicate and fragile even when it is first sown, therefore great care must be taken.

Please note, this holds true for every demonstration of love. However, in this context we are specifically looking at Agape Love, the God kind of Love.

No one could ever be more loving than God Our Father. He is love! It is not simply something He does. With that in mind the initial people group where we have a record of Him showing love, what did those people do? They, as we know disobeyed Him and rejected Him.

At this point there is a universal chorus of gasping and rejection of that assertion because we would never do that!

News Flash we already have.

God is our Father and as such just as with any earthly parent, He accepts we are learning.

Yet, over and over again God has been, is today and will be in the future rejected and disobeyed.

The demonstration of His love is that He never turns away, He doesn't reject us as we repent. At that point we are reinstated into right standing with Him.

An interesting point about God's Love is the nature of it. Agape Love is truly unconditional and even as we may reject it (Prodigal Son), He never stops regardless of our misdeeds.

If the situation was in the natural, many parents

would have turned away and stopped watching for the return of their child. We get hurt to a point that we cannot bear it and put walls up to protect ourselves.

Agape Love is the antipathy of that response. The God kind of love feels the loss, the rejection so deeply that His love grows deeper, stronger, longer.

God's Love never gives up - it never fails!

The Seed for the Nations

The seed of God's love which is planted within each one of us at the moment we yield our lives to Jesus Christ, with correct care will blossom and grow.

I would propose that seed carefully nurtured gives us an ability to love way beyond our natural selves and our natural families and communities. That 'way beyond ability' takes our love in many forms to the nations of the world. If we are sensitive to the whispering of God, He will quicken a nation or a people group which may become a passion project (love) for us.

This Agape Love gives us the ability to acknowledge our differences and yet really see others as God sees them, as He saw each one of us when we were formed in our mothers' wombs.

It allows us to see destiny in them. Not necessarily huge foretelling prophecy, it gives just that profound promise that each one of us has when we give our lives to Jesus. It's the promise of a future and a hope. It is the promise of eternal life. As we go on with Jesus and we learn more, the promise is that we would be in health and prosper even as our soul propers.

> *Beloved, I pray that in all respects you may prosper and be in good health, just as your soul prospers. 3 John 1:2.*

For further encouragement, read the following scripture.

> *Now these are the words of the letter which Jeremiah the prophet sent from Jerusalem to the rest of the elders of the exile, the priests, the prophets, and all the people whom Nebuchadnezzar had taken into exile from Jerusalem to Babylon. (This was after King Jeconiah and the queen mother, the high officials, the leaders of Judah and Jerusalem, the craftsmen, and the metalworkers had departed from Jerusalem.) The letter was sent by the hand of Elasah the son of Shaphan and Gemariah the son of Hilkiah, whom Zedekiah king of Judah sent to Babylon to Nebuchadnezzar king of Babylon, saying, "This is what the LORD of armies, the God of Israel, says to all the exiles whom I have sent into exile from Jerusalem to Babylon:*

'Build houses and live in them; and plant gardens and eat their produce. Take wives and father sons and daughters, and take wives for your sons and give your daughters to husbands, so that they may give birth to sons and daughters; and grow in numbers there and do not decrease. Seek the prosperity of the city where I have sent you into exile, and pray to the LORD in its behalf; for in its prosperity will be your prosperity.'

For this is what the LORD of armies, the God of Israel says: 'Do not let your prophets who are in your midst or your diviners deceive you, and do not listen to their interpretations of your dreams which you dream. For they prophesy falsely to you in My name; I have not sent them,' declares the LORD.

"For this is what the LORD says: 'When seventy years have been completed for Babylon, I will visit you and fulfill My good word to you, to bring you back to this place. For I know the plans that I have for you,' declares the LORD, 'plans for prosperity and not for disaster, to give you a future and a hope. Then you will call upon Me and come and pray to Me, and I will listen to you. And you will seek Me and find Me when you search for Me with all your

heart. I will let Myself be found by you,' declares the LORD, 'and I will restore your fortunes and gather you from all the nations and all the places where I have driven you,' declares the LORD, 'and I will bring you back to the place from where I sent you into exile.'
Jeremiah 29:1-14

56 THE SEED OF LOVE

CHAPTER 6

Love Dismantles The Works Of The Enemy

Love completely disarms the enemy, he has no proficient defence against love. Love allows the light of heaven to shine into the dark places, uncovering the designs, deceptions and strategies of the enemy.

Greater love has no man than he would lay down his life for his friend.

For most of us our love has limits. Of course I can hear you now disagreeing very loudly with that statement, but stay with me.

I know most people saved or unsaved would gladly give their lives for their children perhaps even for a spouse, parent or sibling. Consider this, if someone who is not yet a Christian would lay down their life for one of those I have listed above, how are we different? If we hypothetically are only prepared to do what the world would do, how are we different?

Has the revelation of Jesus in our heart made a difference? Are we fulfilling the scripture?

Here's a thought; it is generally understood and accepted that for us as believers Jesus is our model, and we would therefore endeavour to live as He lived.

The enemy's major weapons are as stated below:

> *Now the deeds of the flesh are evident, which are: sexual immorality, impurity, indecent behavior, idolatry, witchcraft, hostilities, strife, jealousy, outbursts of anger, selfish ambition, dissensions, factions, envy, drunkenness, carousing, and things like these, of which I forewarn you, just as I have forewarned you, that those who practice such things will not inherit the kingdom of God.* Galatians 5:19-21

They are if you look carefully into them all the antipathy of love. Hatred, anger, envy, murder and so on. So in order to dismantle his weapons and completely disarm him we must come in the opposite spirit and that my friends is LOVE.

You know as we grow and mature in our faith we come to understand that it's not about jumping up and down and yelling at the devil. As we behave like that we really are playing his game. We need to become the embodiment of the fruit of the Spirit which is the nature of Christ. The more we have the character of Christ the more freely we move in the power and the authority of Christ.

Remembering always - Jesus Christ already vanquished satan and his cohorts, and He did that on our behalf so we stand in that victory.

This all comes back to, who am I? What are my foundations? Who am I in relation to Christ? Do I believe in my very core what the Bible says about me?

Once we are firm in our answers to those questions the Seed of Love is established within us and with care it will continue to grow and flourish.

CHAPTER 7

It's A Choice

We have talked about planting seeds of love and seeing them miraculously flourish. Let me tell you that's all true yet not inevitable.

There's a wild card if you will in this perfect plan and it's us!

As we read the scripture you can see the promises of God usually have a condition applied to the manifestation of the promise.

Here's a simple example: God promises us eternal life - the condition is that we believe in the truth that Jesus is the Christ. That is what many in the world see as unfair. The question that is often asked is, 'Why doesn't everyone go to heaven?'

Heaven and eternal joy has been prepared for those who love Jesus. The truth we see over and over in scripture is good works (in the world's eyes) will not ensure a place in heaven.

This is what 1 Corinthians 13:3 is talking about.

And if I give away all my possessions to charity, and if I surrender my body so that I may glory, but do not have love, it does me no good.

You can do all sorts of good things but if you do not have love… The problem with this is that we can do good things - clothe the naked, feed the hungry, give help to the poor etc. The important note here is WE CAN DO! In those situations we can and often have completely ignored our need for God.

Now I am not saying that we should not do good things - of course we should. However, our good deeds should be our expression of the Agape Love of the Father flowing through us. That we would do these things and no one other than the God Head knows that we did it. We do not need applause or accolades on an earthly level.

Our need for acknowledgment is recognition of the worlds standards. Please note the wording there that is to say it is possibly more important what the world thinks of us rather than what The Father, Son and Holy Spirit do.

There is nothing wrong with being acknowledged recognised for something. The issue is our need for it.

And that my friends is our choice! I encourage you look at this in your own life and you may come back and say not true I am completely selfless and that's wonderful.

That need is a very sneaky root of pride. Pride was what saw satan being given his marching orders out of heaven. Pride will ensure your ability to love is limited. Think about it, no one can possibly be as gifted, talented or generous as you. You know all this because pride told you so. If that is your point of reference your love will always be patronising and superior.

On that point as we read this book, as we read the word the loudest voice will be telling us we know all about and indeed practice at all times Agape Love. If that is in fact truth you are a very rare human being. Most of us need to learn and discipline our emotions in the ways of God's love.

All the works of the flesh will stymie Agape Love. We may well manifest the other categories of Love however Agape Love is the force that changes everything.

Our choice is do we continue to walk in the fleshly pursuits that comfort us and indeed make us feel great, perhaps in the short term? More seriously does jealousy drive us to a place that can have devastating consequences? (Please don't think that can't happen to us because it can.)

Or do we embrace the promises of God and live our lives wrapped in His Love?

How often have we sadly seen men (and women) of God totally and publicly disgraced because they chose the flesh rather than the Spirit. They chose a different kind of 'love', a poor imitation if you like.

This truth is so important it is related twice in Proverbs.

> *There is a way that seems right to a man, But its end is the way of death.* Proverbs 14:12 NKJV

> *There is a way that seems right to a man, But its end is the way of death.* Proverbs 16:25 NKJV

We should, no we must be sobered by those truths. We are all so clever and in regard to our intellectual knowledge our voice is the loudest one in our head. That voice always seems to tell us what we want to hear. But is it God's voice?

The wide and smooth path is always more appealing and as humans we don't like pain so the narrow steep path is not generally the one everyone is rushing to follow.

Now I can tell you that in my experience the narrow path is where I have always learned the most and the quickest. That's the choice!

I am not saying the wide, smooth path will not get you where God wants you - that's not up to me to judge. I would encourage each one of us to let Holy Spirit be our guide, that's one of reasons He was sent to us.

So how do we know if we're making wise or foolish choices. I would once again direct you to Romans 12, especially verse 2;

> *And do not be conformed to this world, but be transformed by the renewing of your mind, that you may prove what is that good and acceptable and perfect will of God.* Romans 12:2 NKJV

Renew your mind, read the word! When you read it meditate on it and let Holy Spirit reveal what this precious love letter from heaven is saying personally to you.

That in itself, is a choice! Let us ask Holy Spirit to teach us how to love unconditionally, let's make the best choice!

66 THE SEED OF LOVE

CHAPTER 8

Nothing Is Impossible

As I was pondering the subject matter of this book, I believe Holy Spirit began to show me how every facet of our lives is knitted carefully together by the Agape Love of God.

We have often viewed various parts of us as insular.

Faith for example is believing and that's it so move on.

Words of knowledge and wisdom, healing, deliverance, prosperity, prophecy and miracles - we have tended to see as neat little parcels that were accessed independently of one another.

Then as I looked closer and I am sure many of you have seen a relationship between faith and healing for instance. God clearly showed me the tapestry of His great Love for us, and that Love is touching every part of our lives. Our lives as believers wouldn't even be if not for the great Love of God.

The Love that God pours out upon us enables us to function in our calling. It enables us to fulfil vision and ultimately our destiny.

We cannot accomplish anything successfully in our own strength - remember the guys that had a spectacular idea to build a tower to touch heaven, a monument to themselves that would make their name great. God came down, confused their language and scattered them across the earth.

> *Now all the earth used the same language and the same words. And it came about, as they journeyed east, that they found a plain in the land of Shinar and settled there. Then they said to one another, "Come, let's make bricks and fire them thoroughly." And they used brick for stone, and they used tar for mortar. And they said, "Come, let's build ourselves a city, and a tower whose top will reach into heaven, and let's make a name for ourselves; otherwise we will be scattered abroad over the face of all the earth." Now the LORD came down to see the city and the tower which the men had built. And the LORD said, "Behold, they are one people, and they all have the same language.*

And this is what they have started to do, and now nothing which they plan to do will be impossible for them. Come, let Us go down and there confuse their language, so that they will not understand one another's speech." So the LORD scattered them abroad from there over the face of all the earth; and they stopped building the city. Therefore it was named Babel, because there the LORD confused the language of all the earth; and from there the LORD scattered them abroad over the face of all the earth. Genesis 11:1-9

God didn't do that because He was mean or hateful, rather He knew this would destroy them as they had completely left Him out of it. In essence you could say they had no need of God and therefore worshipped themselves. Unfortunately we can look around today and see that same attitude.

The good news is in Chapter 12:1-3 of Genesis, God gets a hold of a man of great integrity called Abram. He gives him a promise that travels through the ages to us today.

Now the LORD said to Abram, "Go from your country, And from your relatives And from your father's house, To the land which I will show you; And I will make you into a great nation, And I will bless you, And make your name great; And you shall be a blessing; And I will bless those who bless you, And the one who curses you I will curse. And in you all the families of the earth will be blessed." Genesis 12:1-3

Of particular note is; **'And I will bless you, And make your name great.'** The very thing the men were trying to do by building their great city and tower. Here God is making that promise to Abram because of his trust in God.

As I have said, because I believe it - the Bible is a love letter from the throne of God to us individually. So you may insert your name instead of the name of whichever man or woman God was addressing. It is for us to personalise His promises. They were all given from His great Love for us, so let's claim them!

What I am trying to show here is nothing of God exists outside of His Love. No matter what the call is on us, no matter whatever office or giftings we may move in, none of it exists outside of His Love for us.

That Love is poured out on the entirety of His creation.

"For God so loved the world, that He gave His only Son... John 3:16

Yes, He loves all. He gave Jesus for all, even those

who shun Him have the same redemptive gifts. They just choose to operate them from a different source. In that operation they are always inferior - counterfeit if you like. In any sort of counterfeit there is always a flaw, it is never as good as the original.

However, as we trust the Lord and don't lean on our own understanding, as we love and worship Him and are mindfully thankful, His love gifts will operate through us with power for His glory.

CHAPTER 9

Eternal Life

When we made that decision to accept Jesus did we at that point make the decision to make Him, allow Him to be Lord of our lives?

Often times that is not the case. Many people have had that come to Jesus moment in a church service which is wonderful. What I would like to address is often the emotionalism of that encounter. Its not always the case however it is something we should be aware of.

Many people accept Jesus because they are fearful of going to hell. As an evangelist friend of ours used to say, 'they are buying fire insurance!' Funny? Sure. There is however a reality and that is if you have an insurance policy, in order for it to remain current you must pay the premiums.

What does that mean in this context? I propose that as important as that moment of encounter was there has to be a life time of God choices following that up.

Does that mean people don't go to heaven? I believe their name is written in the lambs book of life so they will go to that eternal rest. Jesus Himself told us the Kingdom is at hand - it is the kingdom of God.

Everything that our covenantal relationship with Christ has given us access to is right at hand. The choice is ours as to whether we grab it and live in it or look from afar.

In Deuteronomy 34:1-4, The Lord allowed Moses to see the promised land but did not allow him to enter and partake of it.

> *Now Moses went up from the plains of Moab to Mount Nebo, to the top of Pisgah, which is opposite Jericho. And the LORD showed him all the land, Gilead as far as Dan, and all Naphtali and the land of Ephraim and Manasseh, and all the land of Judah as far as the western sea, and the Negev and the territory in the Valley of Jericho, the city of palm trees, as far as Zoar. Then the LORD said to him, "This is the land which I swore to Abra-*

ham, Isaac, and Jacob, saying, 'I will give it to your descendants'; I have let you see it with your eyes, but you will not go over there." Deuteronomy 34:1-4

I pray his experience would not be ours rather we would have that Joshua spirit that will go up and take possession of the promises of God.

The land that was promised to Abraham, Isaac and Jacob is our promise. We are the seed of Abraham. We are the recipients of the blessings of God that were promised to Abram. It is our choice once again as to whether we claim them.

The portion of scripture in Genesis 12:1-3 (refer pg 69) is evidence of God's great overwhelming love for us that has come down through the generations.

Regardless of whatever sins we ourselves or our ancestors may or may not have committed the great Agape Love of God has made provision (through repentance) for us to access all areas of His kingdom.

As we allow the great Agape Love of God to infuse us we can experience;

Every good gift and every perfect gift is from above, and comes down from the Father of lights, with whom there is no variation or shadow of turning. James 1:17 NKJV

God is good and His divine and perfect love for us never changes or falters.

THE SEED OF LOVE

CHAPTER 10

The Last Word

What I am going to say now is too simple and you will probably laugh however I believe it needs to be said.

Two questions you are probably askng now are: How do I learn this? How do I get the right seed?

The very simple answer is read your Bible. Search the Word, seek understanding and revelation.

The more you know the Word and remembering the Word is Jesus, Love will be infused into you. As you open yourself to this, deep hurts will be healed and Love can enter in.

The more you get to know Jesus and fall in love with Him, things really start to change. One of the big changes is Jesus, because of the cross (His death and resurrection) will reconnect you with Father God.

This is huge because God is Love. Just resting in Him will teach you more about Love than you could ever learn in any other way.

The Bible, I believe is a personal love letter from The Father to you and I. The words the prophet Jeremiah spoke sums it up.

> *The LORD appeared to him long ago, saying, "I have loved you with an everlasting love; Therefore I have drawn you out with kindness.*
> Jeremiah 31:3

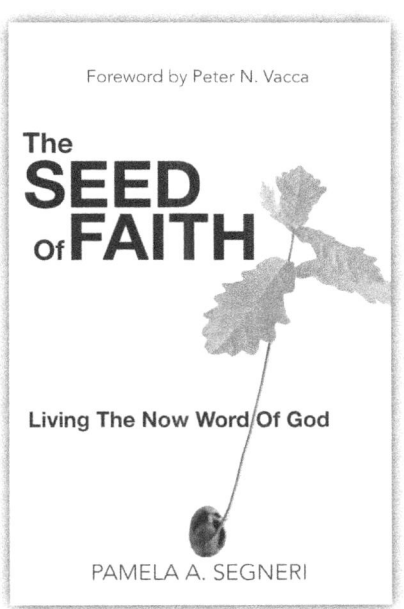

Faith is perhaps the simplest and most difficult discipline we ever have to master. I love that old saying, "from little acorns great oak trees grow". Those acorns are a metaphorical representation of our seed of faith. From those humble seed beginnings we grow and become all that we can be in God.

This is written to inspire and encourage.

The Seed of Faith…. it is in you!

www.theseedoffaithbook.com

The question for us as we face our mountain sometimes in the valley of indecision - do I face down this thing or do I enjoy my quiet unremarkable life? The answer is of course the same - they are simply there and they are not moving of their own volition. As we progress through this journey you will find you have the authority to command them to move. It is entirely our call which challenge we conquer and which we simply tolerate.

ABOUT THE AUTHOR

Pamela Segneri is the co-founder of Integrity Restoration Ministries Inc and the co-founder and Host of firestartersTV. Her desire is to see you fulfil your God given destiny.

www.integritygroup.org.au

www.firestartersTV.com.au

www.ingramcontent.com/pod-product-compliance
Lightning Source LLC
Chambersburg PA
CBHW071837290426
44109CB00017B/1839